P9-DGD-781

Coins

BY DANA MEACHEN RAU

READING CONSULTANT: SUSAN NATIONS, M.ED., AUTHOR/LITERACY COACH/CONSULTANT

WR WEEKLY READER

EARLY LEARNING LIBRARY

Please visit our web site at: **www.earlyliteracy.cc**
For a free color catalog describing Weekly Reader® Early Learning Library's list
of high-quality books, call 1-877-445-5824 (USA) or 1-800-387-3178 (Canada).
Weekly Reader® Early Learning Library's fax: (414) 336-0164.

Library of Congress Cataloging-in-Publication Data

Rau, Dana Meachen, 1971–
    Coins / by Dana Meachen Rau.
        p. cm. — (Money and banks)
    Includes bibliographical references and index.
    ISBN 0-8368-4868-3 (lib. bdg.)
    ISBN 0-8368-4875-6 (softcover)
    1. Coins—United States—Juvenile literature. I. Title. II. Series.
CJ1830.R38   2005
332.4′042′0973—dc22   2005042248

This edition first published in 2006 by
Weekly Reader® Early Learning Library
A Member of the WRC Media Family of Companies
330 West Olive Street, Suite 100
Milwaukee, WI 53212 USA

Editor: Barbara Kiely Miller
Art direction: Tammy West
Cover design and page layout: Dave Kowalski
Picture research: Diane Laska-Swanke

Picture credits: Cover, title, pp. 4, 7, 11, 16, 19 Gregg Andersen; pp. 5, 6, 12, 13, 14, 15,
17, 18, 20, 21 Diane Laska-Swanke; pp. 8, 9, 10 Dave Kowalski/© Weekly Reader Early
Learning Library

Printed in the United States of America

1 2 3 4 5 6 7 8 9 09 08 07 06 05

Table of Contents

Coins make a clinking sound when you drop them into a piggy bank. Coins are a type of currency. **Currency** is the kind of money people use. In the United States, we use dollars as our currency. One dollar is made up of one hundred cents. Coins are cents.

Some children save their coins in a piggy bank.

Coins are made in six different amounts. The one-cent coin is called a penny. The five-cent coin is a nickel. The ten-cent coin is a dime. The twenty-five-cent coin is a quarter. The fifty-cent coin is a half-dollar. Two different coins are each worth one hundred cents. One of them is the golden dollar.

Penny

Nickel

Dime

Quarter

Half-dollar

Golden dollar

A penny looks brown. Nickels, dimes, quarters, and half-dollars look silver. The golden dollar looks gold. Coins are made of mixtures of metals called **alloys**. The alloys used to make coins are made of different mixtures of copper, zinc, and nickel.

Most U.S. coins are a silver color.

Chapter 2 MAKING CENTS

Coins are made by the United States Mint. The word **mint** means to make coins. The United States Mint makes between sixty-five million and eighty million coins every day! Many machines are needed to make coins.

The U.S. Mint makes coins in Denver and Philadelphia (*left*). You can visit the Mint to see how coins are made.

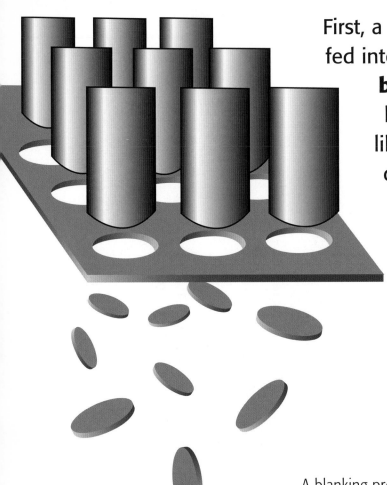

First, a flat sheet of metal is fed into a machine called a **blanking press**. The blanking press works like a cookie cutter. It cuts small, coin-sized circles out of the metal. These circles are called **blanks**. They are the size and shape of coins, but there are no pictures on them.

A blanking press cuts metal into circles.

8

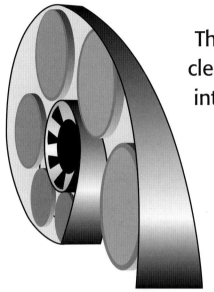

The blanks are heated and cleaned. Then they are put into an upsetting machine. This machine raises the edges of the blanks. The higher edge will help keep the coins from wearing out.

An upsetting machine puts a raised edge around each blank.

The blanks now go into the coining press. This machine stamps pictures on both sides of the blanks. Then an inspector checks each coin to make sure it is perfect. The new coins are counted and poured into bags. The bags of new coins are sent to banks all across the country.

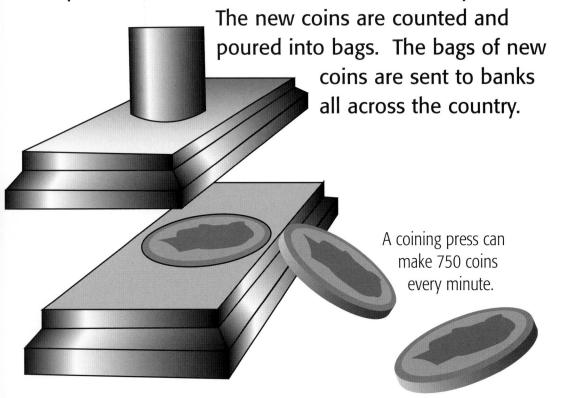

A coining press can make 750 coins every minute.

Have you ever flipped a coin to help you make a decision or a choice? The front of a coin is called heads. The back of a coin is called tails. If the coin lands heads up, you might choose vanilla ice cream. If it lands tails up, you might choose chocolate.

Flipping a coin can help you make a choice.

11

Abraham Lincoln

Thomas Jefferson

Franklin D. Roosevelt

George Washington

John F. Kennedy

Sacagawea

The front sides of most coins have **portraits**, or pictures, of presidents from the past on them. A portrait of Abraham Lincoln is on the penny. The nickel, dime, quarter, and half-dollar coins show presidents, too. The golden dollar has a portrait of Sacagawea. She was a Native American woman. She helped explorers in early America.

The backs of coins have pictures of American symbols or government buildings. The Lincoln Memorial is on the back of the penny. An eagle is on the back of the half-dollar. In 2005, the government made new nickels. Some of them show an American **bison**, or buffalo, on the back. Some show a picture of the Pacific Ocean.

Buildings and animals are shown on the backs of some coins.

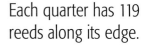
Each quarter has 119 reeds along its edge.

All coins except the penny and the nickel have grooves along their edges. These grooves are called **reeds**. The reeds help people who are blind tell coins apart. The penny and the dime are about the same size. The dime has reeds, but the penny does not.

Each coin shows the date it was made and its amount. All coins also show the word **"Liberty,"** which means freedom. They all say "United States of America" and "In God We Trust." On every coin are the Latin words "E Pluribus Unum," which mean "out of many, one."

"In God We Trust"

"Liberty"

"United States of America"

"E Pluribus Unum"

Coins are small, but they have lots of words on them.

Do you save your coins in a piggy bank to spend later? Some people collect coins that they never plan to spend. Some coin collectors keep their coins safe in envelopes. Others use albums or folders made just for coins.

This boy keeps the coins that he collects in a special folder. The folder has a spot for each coin.

Many coins are no longer minted. They may be worth a lot of money, especially if they are in good shape. Some old coins were made of real gold and silver. Many people like to collect coins from other countries. They can learn a lot about a country and its history from its coins.

Many people collect coins that are no longer made.

You can learn about U.S. states from their quarters.

Some people collect state quarters, too. In 1998, the United States Mint started making new quarters. Over ten years, it will make fifty new kinds of quarters. One quarter is being made for each of the fifty states. The fronts of all the state quarters will look the same. The backs will all be different. The backs will have pictures of something each state is famous for.

Check the coins in your piggy bank. Do you have the quarter for your state?

If you have the quarter for your state, you may want to save it.

Penny = 1 cent   **Nickel = 5 cents**   **Dime = 10 cents**

Look at the coins below. Think about how much each group of coins is worth. Are the coins on the left more than (>), equal to (=), or less than (<) the coins on the right? You can find the correct answers on page 23.

1.

2.

Quarter = 25 cents

Half-dollar = 50 cents

3.

4.

5.

21

Glossary

alloys – mixtures of two or more different metals

blanks – circle-shaped pieces of metal that will become coins

currency – the type of money that is used in a country

inspector – a person who checks coins or other things to make sure they have been made correctly

mint – to make coins

portraits – pictures of people's heads and faces

reeds – the grooves along the edge of some coins

symbols – things that stand for or represent other things

For More Information

Books

Coin Collecting for Kids. Steve Otfinoski
(Innovative Kids)

The Coin Counting Book. Rozanne Lanczak Williams
(Charlesbridge Publishing)

Pennies. Welcome Books (series). Mary Hill
(Children's Press)

Web Sites

The Quarter Craze
library.thinkquest.org/CR0212420/main.htm
Learn all about the new quarters and the states
they represent

The U.S. Mint for Kids
www.usmint.gov/kids/
Fun facts to learn about and games to play with coins

Math Connection Answers: 1) > 2) < 3) > 4) = 5) < 23

Index

About the Author

Dana Meachen Rau is an author, editor, and illustrator. She has written more than one hundred books for children, including nonfiction, early readers, and historical fiction. She lives with her family in Burlington, Connecticut.